Principles and Art
of
Singing

Olga Averino, circa 1975

Principles and Art
of
Singing

Revised Edition

Olga Averino

Edited by
Irina Lasoff

Edited by Irina Lasoff
Text design by Elizabeth E. Tustian
Cover design by Clemens Bergfeld

Forlaget Intention
c/o Institut for F.M. Alexander'sTeknik
20 Solmarksvej
Aarhus, Denmark

ISBN 87-89389-01-8

Printed in Denmark
by N. Olaf Møller

Contents

Olga Averino, circa 1933

Foreword

Olga Averino was born to a musical family in Moscow in 1895. Her father, Nicholas Averino, was a violist and Director of the Imperial Conservatory in Rostov. Her mother, Olga Laroche, daughter of the musical critic Hermann Laroche and goddaughter of Peter Tchaikovsky, was a pianist. Mme. Averino herself was the goddaughter of Modest Tchaikovsky, the composer's brother. From an early age she was surrounded by music, and at the age of five, she began her musical training on the piano. She was also taken to the concerts and heard the rehearsals of family friends, such as Josef Lhévinne, Feodor Chaliapin, Alexander Scriabin, Alexander Siloti, and Sergei Rachmaninoff. When she later graduated from the Imperial Conservatory in Saratov in piano and voice, she had the excellent technique and musicianship that the conservatory demanded and her standards of performance had been set by her early musical experiences.

In Russia and later in the Far East, Mme. Averino sang the principal roles in many operas. These were not easy times. Revolution and civil war forced her and her husband, the violinist Paul Fedorovsky, with their small daughter, Irina, to flee Russia across Siberia to Vladivostok and eventually to China. There was hunger, disrupted transportation, and the advances and retreats of fighting armies. At the age of twenty-three, she was diagnosed with tuberculosis and given only three years to live. Perhaps through sheer strength of will, she survived and lived another seventy. But these turbulent times had their odd and funny moments. Vladivostok in those days was overflowing with refugees and soldiers, heroes and entrepreneurs, and former political prisoners and criminals, who had served their time in the Siberian prisons. In later years, Mme. Averino often entertained students and friends with stories of the characters and criminals whom she had met in those days and of singing in operas with make-shift costumes and almost no scenery, because the director had pawned everything he could to settle his gambling debts. She also told of the strangeness, poverty, and beauty of China in the twenties.

In 1924, Mme. Averino arrived in New York City where she once more met the pianist Alexander Siloti, Liszt's last pupil. The families had been friends in Russia, and now respect and admiration led to friendship and a close musical association that was to last many years. She was the only singer whom Mr. Siloti ever offered to accompany, and she was chosen by him in 1936 to sing in his last public concerts, which commemorated the fiftieth anniversary of his teacher's death.

In 1925, Mme. Averino moved to Boston, where her husband had taken a position with the Boston Symphony. At the same time, she was reunited with her father who had also joined the same orchestra. By this time, she had turned to a career in the repertoire of recitals and oratorios, for she had found that the second rate quality of most opera productions — the singers, orchestra, chorus, and corps du ballet included — did not interest her.

Mme. Averino made her New York City debut in Town Hall on October 30, 1929, the day before Black Thursday. She was always amused by the juxtaposition of the headlines the next morning: "Russian Soprano, Olga Averino, Sings Debut Recital," "Stock Market Closes." But her debut was indeed a noteworthy event. She sang a varied program of Russian, French, and English music that included little-known works of Tchaikovsky and Ravel's Chansons Madécasses. This was the second New York performance of the piece and was highly praised, all the more so in comparison with the first performance, for which the composer himself had played. Olin Downes, the critic for the *New York Times*, wrote:

> Mme. Averino sang the Ravel *Chansons Madécasses*, which, when previously performed in this city, had seemed idle, futile and manufactured music. Lo! the singer gave these songs an atmosphere and significance which revealed them as among the most interesting of Ravel's late scores. And here her voice had a beauty and variety of effect which revealed all its inherent capacities for line and expression. It is a voice full of individuality and essentially rich in color, and it is an [expression] of the personality and artistic intentions of the singer. In Ravel's music, . . . [the voice] had a haunting sonority and variety of nuance, and there was excellent execution of trills, passage work and other technical problems. In the lower register the voice is particularly warm. The upper part was now employed with highly dramatic result. The

Chansons Madécasses were thus laden with half subtle, half
barbaric meanings. When text and tone were combined, there
was the most eloquent recitation. When tone alone was
employed, on certain wordless sounds, it said more than text,
beginning indeed where text left off, fulfilling the meaning
which speech only half revealed.*

Such praises as these were to be repeated again and again
throughout her concert career. She was a superb stylist and
at all times restrained her ego so that the music could speak
for itself. Her musical intelligence and sensitivity to the text
were often noted. Mme. Averino had little tolerance for the
indulgence of personality at the cost to music, and a beautiful
sound with no appropriate feeling behind it meant little to
her. Her programs always roused interest, for they were
varied and broad. She was equally at home with early music
and modern music, as well as the familiar repertoire of the
eighteenth and nineteenth centuries. Early music she often
performed with her husband, a founding member of the
Boston Society for Early Music. And as for modern music,
she sang the American premiere of Berg's "Lied der Lulu"
with the Boston Symphony under Serge Koussevitsky and
worked with the composers Glazounoff, Rachmaninoff, and
Stravinsky. She also toured with Pizzetti and sang the music
of Schoenberg, Hindemith and others.

In the years that followed, Mme. Averino's name became
closely associated with that of the Boston Symphony. Among
the works she performed with Dr. Koussevitsky were
Beethoven's Ninth Symphony, Bach's B-Minor Mass, De-

---

*Mme. Averino was always proud of the fact that all her reviews could be
reprinted in their entirety. I must therefore apologize to her spirit: I have
excerpted only for the sake of brevity.

bussy's *The Martyrdom of Saint Sebastian*, Ravel's *Shéhérazade*, and the Letter Scene from Tchaikovsky's *Eugene Onegin*. According to her count, she had twenty-seven engagements with that orchestra under Serge Koussevitsky, who wrote of her:

> Mme. Averino possesses a voice of exceptional beauty over which she has a marvelous control. Her deep understanding of the music she sings, her insight into the different styles, the delicate shading and moulding of phrases bear evidence of her extraordinary musicianship. Indeed, in her interpretation each composition lives, keeps its distinctive style and colouring. These rare qualities distinguish Mme. Averino and place her in the foremost rank of the vocal artists of to-day.

Mme. Averino's appearance with musical organizations was not limited to the Boston Symphony. She sang as a soloist with symphony orchestras in cities such as Washington, Detroit, Montréal, Chicago, Pittsburg, Philadelphia, Worcester, and Springfield. She sang in the Coolidge Festivals in Chicago, Pittsfield, and Washington. Performing the Schoenberg Second String Quartet, she toured with the Pro Arte String Quartet. She also sang this piece with the London, Gordon, and Kolisch string quartets.

As a recitalist Mme. Averino sang frequently at Town Hall in New York City and appeared in many major American cities. She also toured with the cellist Gregor Piatigorsky. She sang at the League of Composers. At the height of her career, she had to refuse offers of foreign tours since her legal status did not allow her to leave the United States.

Although she began tapering off the number of her appearances in the 1950s, it was not until 1971, at the age of 76, that Mme. Averino sang her last full recital. As she began giving fewer public performances, she devoted more of herself to her teaching career. Even after her last recital, she would often sing for her students in her master classes, which she continued to hold until a year before her death in 1989 at the age of 93.

Mme. Averino had begun her teaching career in China in the twenties. It was a multi-lingual experience, to say the least. She would speak French during an Englishwoman's lesson in which the student sang an Italian song. Then she would speak pidgin Chinese with her daughter's Ama, pidgin English with the man servant, and German with the cook. By the time evening came, she could barely utter a word of Russian to her family.

When she came to America, she continued to teach, and in 1938, she became head of the Voice Department at the Longy School of Music in Cambridge, Massachusetts. From 1941 to 1950, she also taught at Wellesley College. From 1938 to 1940, she was a guest artist and teacher at the Middlebury Music Center in Vermont. In the 1960s, she gave many workshop-lectures on principles of singing for various groups: The Harvard Lutheran Choral Society, Harvard University Choir, American Guild of Organists, and the Institute of Church Music at Colby College in Maine. In 1976, already in her eighties, she left the Longy School to help found the New School of Music under the directorship of Nicholas Van Slyck.

Mme. Averino always held her students to the highest of professional standards, even if their aspirations were but modest. Although she knew that only a small number of the many hundreds of pupils whom she taught would become professionals, she felt that it was important to educate audiences as well as performers. Students who took her training to heart came to understand the musician's and performer's art. And if they complained that they no longer got as much pleasure out of concerts as they used to, she would reply that the pleasure they would get from truly fine performances was just so much the greater.

Although the training of her students might almost be called severe, Mme. Averino's sympathies for their vocal problems were great. As she describes in her personal history, she had many difficulties learning to sing, and the process of self-teaching that ensued gave her the requisite patience and understanding of a master teacher. Mme. Averino's understanding extended beyond the strictly vocal. Her students came to her with their personal problems as well. She listened and advised, and even when she admonished a pupil for his actions, she accepted him for who he was. She did this not only out of fondness for her students, but because it was part of her way of training her students. She often stated, "You can't live one thing and sing another." For her, the self-restraint and consideration for others (the composer) necessary for singing were just as necessary in life. Just as you apply all your abilities and consciousness to the act of singing, you apply them to life as well. Mme. Averino never fell into the trap of the unexamined life nor compromised her integrity.

To lead life as she did required courage. And courage she had in no small measure. Her mother died when Mme. Averino was little more than one year old. Afterwards she was cared for by relatives and later a loving step-mother, but she always felt herself alone and independent. The stories she told of her early life showed that she had developed an unusual sense of self and an ability for self observation at a very young age. She fled Russia and never looked back with regret. She left her husband and daughter in China, unsure of when they would follow her, but knowing that life in America would eventually be better for them all. She said no to powerful people who wanted her to sing in performances or pieces in which she did not believe. Although she had some serious and painful illnesses, she did not dwell on them. She was always looking ahead. The past was to learn from or to be entertained by. Already in her eighties, she helped found a new music school, because of her belief in its principles. At the same time, not knowing if she would ever see it published, she began this book in a language not her own, and in her last year of life she began writing her memoirs. Although bed-ridden, she continued teaching and demonstrating to within days of her death. She peacefully passed from this life at home in her own bed.

Singer, teacher, friend, and guide, Olga Averino took pleasure in all aspects of life. She was actively interested in politics and philosophy and amused by stories of friends and acquaintances. She enjoyed watching the skill of professional sportsmen, cooking a special meal for friends, or playing a game of bridge or Chinese checkers. In her later years, the peace of her summer home on Prince Edward Island, Canada, and the many friends she made there were sources of great pleasure to her.

She has, with this book, left us only a part of her life. But it is an essential part. It cannot be read superficially, for it is compact and condensed, filled with the distillation of a life's experience. If Mme. Averino's images seem difficult to understand on first reading, it is because she has described an inner process not easily captured by language. And true understanding will take place only if the reader is able to experience and internalize the process described. In this book, Mme. Averino has given us a high standard to live by, but it is not an impossible standard, for with her life she demonstrated that it was not only possible to attain such standards, but necessary for living a full and conscious life.

Nicholas T. Lasoff
Cambridge, Massachusetts
May 1989

Foreword to the First Edition

Olga Averino was born into a musical family in Moscow before the turn of the century. The goddaughter of Modest Tchaikovsky, she grew up in an environment rich in artistic friends, including Rachmaninoff, Siloti, and Scriabin. She graduated from the Conservatory as a pianist, but changed her post graduate studies there to theory and voice. In 1918 she joined one of the leading Russian opera companies and toured with this group until the Revolution drove her from the country. Traveling with her husband, violinist Paul Fedorovsky, their young daughter and other musicians, she escaped across Siberia to China, and eventually to America.

In 1929, Olga Averino's New York debut took place in Town Hall. The *New York Times* described her voice in that performance in superlatives: rich in color, full of individuality, capable of both dramatic intensity and "haunting sonority." This brilliant beginning was followed by performances in concert halls from Washington to Detroit, from Montréal to Philadelphia, everywhere drawing tremendous public acclaim. Boston audiences had the pleasure of hearing Olga Averino often as soloist with the Boston Symphony, for Boston was her new home, and recitals and concerts throughout New England were always part of her busy schedule.

One critic's prediction, made in 1929, seems particularly apt: "Whatever she does will be imbued with intelligence and musical distinction." In fact, intelligence, distinction, good taste and what another critic called a "spontaneous capacity for expression," characterize not only Olga Averino's stage career, but also her teaching, her writing, and her daily life. For those around her, though, her greatest gift is an unerring ability to see to the core of every situation and to articulate with marvelous clarity exactly what she sees. Objectivity and insight, a boundless interest in each thing for itself, whether it be a song, a play, a child's story, or a scientific fact, are the qualities which differentiate her as an artist, teacher, and friend.

These are the qualities which also serve to make this little book special. It is not about Olga Averino, though her fascinating life would interest many of us. It is about the art of singing itself, viewed from a perspective of a lifetime of listening, performing, and teaching, distilled to very few pages of carefully thought out principles. And like all things which are true, the book is not just about singing but about life, about the forces which enable each of us to reach our potential in the greatest art of all.

Joey Brode
Cambridge, Massachusetts
1984

Author's Acknowledgements

Some years ago, I was asked to give a series of lecture-demonstrations on the principles of singing for the Harvard Lutheran Society. This series was successful and was repeated several times. Similar lectures followed in other colleges and organizations. The participants were as varied as the places in which the lectures were given: singers, teachers, students, organists, and choral conductors. Many of these people asked me to write a book on the subject of my talks. To give lectures, however, with demonstrations of all you say, is one thing. To write a book on the same subject is another. The inherent difficulties of the task led me to resist the demand to write. Then one day, in a state of euphoria, and mostly because of a kind offer to help from my dear friend, Joey Brode, I decided to do it. I am most lucky to have had interest, encouragement, and patience from my family and friends who listened to my first attempts to bring order to such resistant material.

I wish I could say something stronger than just "thank you" for all the interest, moral support, and active help from the following people. The first people who helped after Joey Brode were Claire Smith, Joe Dwyer, Martha Smith, Swami Sarvagatananda, Irina Lasoff, who spent almost as much time helping me as I myself spent on the book, Donalda McLeod, Vicky Wang, and lately Criss and Edwin Taylor, whose help and enthusiasm gave me a much-needed final push.

Several people have asked me, "For whom did you write this book?" This book came to life because my students asked for it. So it is affectionately dedicated to all my pupils, everyone of whom, without exception, taught me valuable lessons.

Olga Averino
Spring 1988

Further Acknowledgements

The family of Madame Averino would like to acknowledge the following people for their contributions to the present edition: Edwin F. Taylor for editing and word processing; Andrew Taylor for page composition; Elizabeth Tustian for text design; Clemens Bergfeld for cover design; Gitte Fjordbo of Intention Publishing for making publication in Denmark possible; Hariklia Gounari of Intention Publishing and Director of the Institut for F. M. Alexander's Teknik, whose initial interest in the book caused it to be published in the Alexander Technique community. We regret that we were unable to identify the photographers. We would especially like to thank Crissman Taylor, without whose unflagging interest and generous help the publication of this book in its present form would not have been possible.

Irina, Benjamin, Michael, Loes, Mark, Susan,
Nicholas, and Barbara Lasoff, May 1989

Principles and Art
of
Singing

1

Singing: An Organic Process

The voice is so complex and the elements which make it up are so interdependent that each time we say one thing, describe one aspect, there seems to be a "yes, but..." lurking somewhere. However, in order to understand the workings of the voice, the analysis of each element that constitutes its proper functioning is helpful. Still, while concentrating on one aspect, we must not lose sight of the whole.

Singing—the use of the voice—is by its nature an organic process. Almost anyone, unless afflicted with some physical or mental handicap, can sing. But when we speak of professional singing, we must examine the specific skills which need to be developed.

Of course there are many natural singers. They come from all walks of life and some have become world famous. Galli-Curci, who took no singing lessons, and Chaliapin, who had little training, were among these gifted people. Natural singers have certain traits in common. All have a vivid imagination, spontaneous nature, and natural physical coordination. Natural singers have a wide voice range and the ability to make clear sounds. There is no noticeable change in registers, the breath is free, the diction clear. Analysis of what happens when people sing well sheds light on the proper functioning of the singing voice.

The process of good singing is a process of physical and psychological coordination. Physical coordination depends on the alignment of the singer's instrument. In itself, it produces no sound, but it creates the conditions which allow the imagination to produce the song. Clearly we must start our investigation of the process of singing with the instrument itself, and here arises our first difficulty.

Ask any singer, "How would you define your voice?" and the response will be one of bewilderment—some vague reference to "myself" or a distracted gesture towards the throat. The voice is invisible and unknown, and yet it is the mysterious instrument which the singer must master in order to make music. Every other musical instrument is outside the self, an object separate from the performer. If it is not in perfect condition, it can be tuned or repaired by a specialist. The voice, however, is merged with the performer, and the distinction between the performer and the instrument is not clear to most people. Who would compliment Jasha Heifetz by saying, "He has a beautiful violin"? Yet how often one hears it said of a singer that "his voice is beautiful."

My hope is that this book will help to clarify some of the mystery and confusion which seems to plague so many singers.

2

A Singer's Personal History

During my first year as a conservatory student (I was then majoring in piano), I noticed that all of the students were divided into two groups. The instrumentalists formed a large group and the singers a smaller one, and there was little communication between them. One obvious reason for the division was that the obligatory theoretical classes for these two groups were different. We instrumentalists had one year of elementary theory, three years of harmony and solfeggio, one year each of orchestration, reading scores, and analysis of form and fugue. Singers had one year of theory and two years of harmony and solfeggio, but instead of orchestration, etc., they had to take languages, dance, and stage movement.

Our group of instrumentalists thought we were better educated as musicians than the singers and felt superior to them. There was another peculiarity: When we talked about our progress and difficulties, we discussed certain methods, amount of time for practicing, memorization, etc. Singers had entirely different concerns. They spoke about some-body's high C, ability or inability to sing pianissimo, success or failure "to put the voice into the mask." They also shared strange problems and sympathized with each other about such things as the inability to sing low notes in the morning or to sing anything before 2 P.M., etc. To instrumentalists, it all sounded incomprehensible and we simply thought all singers were odd.

This attitude changed radically for me when I completed my studies as a pianist and decided to become a singer. Up to that time, all my studies had been easy for me. All I had had to know was what I was supposed to do and why, and I would then find the way to do it well.

At my first singing lesson, I was told to sing in such a way that my voice would fill the empty spaces in my skull, to keep the chest bone high, and to shape the inside of my mouth like a pear. There were some other instructions as well, none of which I understood. My voice was naturally flexible and of a wide range. I had four E's—three octaves—and could imitate other female singers. Because of this and my solid musical background, I was immediately put in an opera class and given the part of Gilda in Verdi's "Rigoletto." I immedi-ately became "a star." It flattered my ego no end, but reason told me it wouldn't last, and it did not. It is one thing to imitate a single phrase sung by a good singer, and it is quite another to sustain without training a demanding part throughout a whole opera.

At the same time I was also trying to incorporate the instructions which had been given to me and which I did not understand. This situation brought about prompt and sad results: I started losing first the top, then the bottom notes, and soon was left with about one octave of sour sounds. I had joined the family of singers.

I will skip the long story of shopping for the right teacher and the long search which happily for me ended well.

I make this side trip into my personal history because I learned much from these early difficulties. In the process of my search, I tapped many sources ranging from anatomy to phonetics and to the yoga disciplines as they related to breath. Had my progress been smooth, there would have been no reason to concern myself with these things. What happened to me was not such a rare occurrence and still happens to singers. Although the vocal instructions I received were obviously not good, my voice teacher had been a renowned singer and a great artist. I suspect he was one of those men who sang "by the grace of God" and could not convey the process in cold words. However, he demonstrated beautifully. The rest of his large class thrived on his demonstrations and most of the students progressed. I was the one, "the star," the literal-minded one who regressed with remarkable speed. This experience was a valuable lesson.

This is the end of the detour, and now we will turn to our main theme—the principles of singing.

3

The Voice: A Unique Instrument

I ask my readers to follow three imaginary music students as they first learn to use their instruments. They are a pianist, a cellist, and a singer; we will examine the essential differences in the way these three students approach their instruments.

Before the first two of these students begin to use their instruments, they are informed as to the nature and function of the piano and the cello, and are given demonstrations. In both cases, in order to produce a desirable sound, the player must find a note corresponding to this sound on his instrument. One has to know the place on the instrument which corresponds to this symbol.

The pianist sees the keyboard before him and learns that if he wants higher-pitched sounds, he has to move his hand on the keyboard to the right, and for lower pitches, to the left. Both hands perform the same function in playing the piano: fingers striking the keys and pressing down into the instrument. For longer duration of sound, the pedal is pressed with the foot. However complicated the technique becomes, the actual function remains the same for both hands.

The cellist's task is different. His left hand finds the notes on the strings but this gives a barely audible sound. The bow must be moved with the right hand across the string in order to produce a continuous sound. The cellist learns that to produce *higher* pitches, his left hand must go *down* on the instrument toward the floor and *up* on the instrument for lower sounds. The bow has several strokes which the cellist must learn. So while the pianist uses both hands to perform the same function on his instrument, the cellist uses each hand for a different function—i.e., he has two different elements to attend to. To produce a perfect melody or even a sound, the cellist must be sure that both elements are working correctly, and it is not too difficult to tell them apart. The sound is the result of the work of the cellist's elements, his tools, and they are different from the tools of the pianist.

But, the training of the cellist and the pianist is alike in one important aspect: both start working gradually, both become acquainted with their instruments, and both learn to handle them. It takes quite a while before either of these musicians can produce simple pleasant music. However, when problems appear it is usually not difficult to ascertain what needs correction.

Let us see what happens to the singer. The vocal instrument cannot be seen. It is impossible to demonstrate what is essential or extraneous to its functioning. Yet a singer can not only make sounds, but quite often sings rather nicely, and can sing a whole song. So what results from considerable work and concentration on the part of the instrumentalist is no problem for the singer. The singer, however, has no idea how this song is actually produced. What is more, if something goes wrong, the singer does not know why it happened or how to correct it.

If you ask singers how they sing, they will usually answer: "I don't know; I just sing." The functioning of the several physiological elements of the voice (the instrument) and of the psychological element (the performer's imagination) which produces the music are so intermingled that the young singer is usually conscious of only one thing, "the voice." There is, however, one strong sensation which is shared by all singers: a sensation which they describe as "the voice moving for the pitch." But unlike the instrumentalists who immediately learn the construction of their instruments and move their hands accordingly, the singer is in the dark about where and what to move and seeing the printed music in front of him, jumps to the conclusion that his "voice" moves up in his throat for the high pitches and down for the lower ones.

Maybe there are some happy exceptions to this false notion among singers, but they must be rare; I haven't met any. I feel that a great many of our vocal troubles stem from this false concept. Let us put the same printed melody in front of our three students. To go from low to high notes, the pianist's hand moves to the left for the low pitch and to the right for the high one. The cellist's left hand moves up for the low pitch and down for the high, but the singer follows the visual line and thinks it is necessary to move up and down with the line of the printed melody. Often singers raise their eyebrows or stand on their toes for high notes and pull their chins down for the low ones. What is more, they do not know what it is that moves up and down. If you ask them, they say, "It is my voice."

In making music, instrumentalists and singers alike deal with notes, but there is one cardinal difference, which in my opinion is never clearly defined, and is, therefore, a source of much confusion. For the instrumentalist, a note has a double meaning: 1) the printed code—a symbol for pitch on a piece of paper; 2) the place on the instrument which corresponds to this symbol. For the singer only the first part—the printed symbol—exists. There is no specific place in the vocal instrument for notes, but consciously or unconsciously, singers behave as if there was one, and this mistaken idea leads them into many difficulties.

The instrumentalist knows where the printed notes are to be found on his instrument. His technique consists in the rapidity and sureness with which his hands can find the keys or positions which correspond to those printed notes. Of course, some instrumentalists, such as string players, naturally hear in their imaginations the sound they want to produce and then find the corresponding note. On highly mechanized instruments like the piano or organ, it is possible to go directly to the note by looking at the instrument, without hearing the note in the mind first. But this is not the case with the singer's instrument. The singer must imagine the desired sound, hear it very clearly, and feel *the urge* to produce it. *This urge is the very essence of vocal sound.* The singer then releases the breath and an audible sound is produced. *This urge together with the inner hearing of the sound tunes our vocal apparatus to the desired pitch without the use of any voluntary (conscious) muscles.*

The purpose of this discussion is to show that singing, unlike the process of making music on other instruments, is a truly organic process. As in any organic process, it represents a coordinated functioning of several components. There are three obvious ones: breath, sound, and speech. These are the singer's tools. Yet there is another element, less obvious, but subtle and extremely powerful, which acts like the battery in a car; without it nothing else can work. Everything we do is the result of this energy and muscles working together. The mind gives an order for action and the nerves carry the energy to the muscles; the muscles can then be trained to do the skillful work.

That is the work process that instrumentalists use. They deal with the voluntary muscles of fingers, arms, and lips, and train them accordingly. But the singer's vocal chords— the source of the audible sound—are involuntary membranes operated directly by energy and therefore they cannot be trained. It is essential to remember this. Because of this fact, vocal technique (and a very precise one) is of a very different kind from that of the instrumentalists. It is energy and imagination that produce the song, but posture, breath, and speech align the instrument. They can help or hinder the singing. The singer who coordinates these elements well and whose imagination works freely is indeed well trained.

The first thing is to realize that the vocal instrument does not belong to the keyboard type. It is impossible "to hit the note"—a notion most prevalent among singers. If anything, the human voice is closer to a wind instrument. The means of making audible sounds is by releasing breath, thus making the vocal cords vibrate. The different pitches are produced by clearly hearing the sound or melody in one's mind and feeling a strong urge to produce it—in a word, using energy-impulse.

The voice which is perceived by the singer as a single moving force is, in reality, the simultaneous functioning of several elements of the vocal apparatus. These elements are the singer's tools. Unlike the instrumentalist, who has used his tools consciously throughout his life, the singer has to become conscious of elements that he has always used without his being aware of their functioning. This is not only an important point; it is a most crucial one and, until it is recognized as such, the confusion like a shadow will follow the singer in his studies. Obviously, the singer's problem and the approach to it is very different from the task of the instrumentalist. The first step for a singer is to become aware of these elusive tools.

4

Impulse (Vital Energy)

Observe the animal world: the flight of a bird, the sureness in the leap of a squirrel from the branch of one tree to another swaying branch, the whine of a puppy, the roar of a lion.

These actions are performed instinctively, without a conscious effort, but they were prompted by some need, some urge. *This urge works like a spark which ignites and releases a stream of energy. The initial urge becomes the goal. Urge and goal seem to be one, and as long as the urge-goal remains strong, the stream of energy lasts.* We see it in everyday action of animals and also in the almost unbelievably mysterious migrations of animals and birds.

I am speaking of subtle, elusive, and all-powerful energy which is present and functions in everyone and everything alive. The French call it *l' elan vital*. The Hindus call it *prana*. In the arts and in medicine, it is referred to as "impulse," so I will use this more familiar term. This vital energy is omnipresent, therefore we tend to take it for granted, like the air we breathe. However, when we witness some special act, we become aware of the presence of something unusual, and if it is a performance of some kind we describe it in vague terms: "the performer surpassed himself," or "he was inspired, " or "it was magic," etc. The influx of vital energy makes the performance "magic." In order to recognize this energy and channel it, one must first become aware of it, of its presence and its function. I hope to make clear what it is by giving some examples of its manifestation.

In human life the first manifestation of impulse is the cry of a newborn baby as he takes his first breath. If you watch the baby's body you will see the abdominal muscles contracting. This is the sign that the diaphragm is working, pushing the air from the lungs toward the vocal cords and making the first natural, "rooted" sound. It is a very important point that the *first manifestation of impulse is through breath.* It is worth noticing how strongly and sometimes how long this baby cries without any sign of hoarseness or fatigue. These first sounds express a strong but undifferentiated urge or need for something, such as food, warmth, or comfort. These sounds change with the growth of the child. They begin to express different and more clearly defined moods—joy, anger, amusement. We notice that the sharper the mood, the stronger the influx of the energy. All of these sounds are produced in the same spontaneous way, always connected with the diaphragm.

The growing child's moods and thoughts become more varied; the child's attention is concentrated on them. This concentration makes the flow of energy very strong. Sometimes children with a very strong influx of this energy are difficult to deal with. We see that where there is intense concentration, there is also a powerful influx of this energy.

Let us look at adults who are able to choose the subject on which to focus their concentration. They can focus it on any level—physical, emotional, mental, esthetic, or spiritual. The most tangible and observable manifestation is on the physical level. A very striking example is the performance of a karate master when he splits wood with the blow of his bare hand, or when his hand crushes a rock.

You see the same energy working (applied differently) in gymnasts, divers, or people who maintain equilibrium in almost impossible situations. One can be sure that when the performance seems "miraculous," it is the result of great concentration and the influx of impulse.

When concentration is not on the physical level, it is not as visible, but you can observe the effect of concentration on an audience. During performances by great artists, musicians, or actors, and during poetic readings or inspired speeches, one becomes aware of the absorbed attention of the audience—that stillness which sometimes continues for a few moments after the performance has ended. Such energy is extremely communicable and, what is more, it has a very long-lasting effect. It is brought home and remembered for a long time.

Impulse is present in everybody, but some people seem to be filled with it; they are vital. Others at times seem to be vital but then become listless. Since this energy is the origin of vocal sound, vitality is the most desirable quality in a singer.

The vital person is the happy possessor of that energy that makes everything seem so easy. I'm sure that at one time or another every singer has had the experience of singing easily, simply, without the difficulties which so often interfere. At such moments, the energy is running high. It is also possible to be very musical and have a pleasant voice, but to have the energy flow only intermittently. It is most important that before singing you put yourself into a state of vitality. How? I have had many conversations with colleagues who agreed and understood the role of this vital energy in singing, but who maintained that it was mystical and inspirational and could not be taught. It *is* mystical and inspirational and, although it cannot be taught, one must still be aware of its presence, and its ebb and flow in order to be able to stimulate it.

Let me demonstrate with an example: you come home tired and listless after a day's work. You have to climb two flights of stairs. Suddenly somebody shouts good news from the top of the stairs. In no time, you are at the head of the stairs, and you no longer feel fatigued. This is the result of the influx of impulse or energy. Do not confuse it with emotion; it is not the same thing. Emotion and many other factors may stimulate this energy, such as the impression made by great beauty or by a marvelous idea or by anything truly important to you. Any of these may serve to create within you the "urge" to sing, may put you "in the mood" for it.

Impulse, or vital energy, may be observed most clearly in the performance of athletes. If you watch gymnasts before they perform, you see tremendous concentration, a gathering of physical and mental forces, a moment of stillness, and then the release of these forces. Among musicians, this energy is most visible in conductors. However, it is possible to be an accomplished musician and still have very little of this vitality. Such a musician may perform with great clarity, skill, and correctness, but the performance will be dry. On the other hand, a conductor filled with "impulse" will give an electrifying performance. That is because this vital energy is completely communicable and contagious.

This state of vitality can be stimulated. Individuals must each find the best way to stimulate impulse for themselves. For some people the best way is to go through physical exercises and raise the vitality of the body. Others are stimulated by something very beautiful—music, some special performance, poetry, or nature. Anything that will induce the wonderful mood of wanting to sing, of being impatient to sing, is helpful. Once in the "mood," you will recognize it. You will feel wonderful, both peaceful and alive, and your full concentration will be focused on the music. I want to emphasize that this influx of vitality is not excitement. To be in a state of excitement is like riding a runaway horse. You are not in control. But with the influx of energy, one feels very peaceful and confident. You are in the same state as the gymnast who is about to perform. All your inner forces are gathered in a moment of intense concentration and then this energy is released into the performance.

We must remember that the newborn baby gave us the first demonstration of a perfect, natural sound, started spontaneously by urge (impulse, used unconsciously) and manifested through diaphragmatic breath. So, now we come to the most pertinent point: how the singer directs this subtle, evasive, and powerful impulse. In using any energy, three points are of extreme importance:

1) *The starting point of the energy:*
   For the singer, this point is the clear imagining of the musical phrase combined with the strong urge to sing it (the mystical and inspirational aspect of impulse, which works like a spark).

2) *The channel through which the energy travels:*
For the singer, the actual release of this energy through the singer's channel (diaphragmatic breath) and allowing it to flow uninterruptedly upward and always in through the larynx and vocal cords.

3) *The location of the goal or the receiving point of energy:*
For the singer, reaching the pharynx—the singer's main resonator.

The coordinated use of all these elements is the core of the vocal process.

In a previous chapter, I said: ". . .the impulse tunes the instrument (vocal cords) to the desired pitch." It also releases and controls the breath and vitalizes the working parts of the vocal apparatus. It must be obvious how important the role of this energy is in the vocal process. Equally, and perhaps even more importantly, is the manifestation of this energy on the mental level.

In this chapter, we discussed impulse only as a tool. We will return to impulse in Chapter 8, "The Art of Singing," and talk about its other aspects.

5

Breath

Impulse is a very important factor in any performance. In singing it is the *most* important one, for not only is it the source of sound, it is also the means of controlling the breath. Whenever there is continuity of sound, there is also movement. In singing it is the breath that moves. Our aim as singers is to establish a smooth flow of breath that travels from the lower part of the lungs up through the larynx and vocal cords and fills the pharynx, the cavity at the top and back of the throat. The pharynx is our resonator.

We can deliberately stop breathing for a short time and then begin again, but the continuous breathing that goes on throughout life is unconscious. We breathe best while we sleep, but this obviously is of no help to the singer. How to take conscious control over a function best done unconsciously is the problem. Its solution lies in the interaction of impulse and breath. Impulse tunes the vocal cords to the desired pitch, but to make the pitch audible, it is necessary to let air—our breath—pass through the cords, causing them to vibrate. So the steady upward flow of breath is extremely important.

All our natural sounds, crying, laughing, coughing, are "rooted" sounds, that is, they are strongly connected with the diaphragm. If you circle your waist with your hands and cough or laugh, you will feel the muscles of the abdomen contract under your fingers (the same muscles you observed contracting in a crying baby). This is the "rooted" diaphragmatic sound. It is of the utmost importance for singers to use a *rooted* sound at all times. Much depends on how the breath is taken. Do not consciously try to take a slow breath or take a great deal of air through either the nose or mouth alone. Such methods are not very helpful because they create tension. The intake of breath should be comfortable: inhale partly through the mouth, partly through the nose as you do in everyday life. Do not take in too much air, and try to fill only the lower part of your lungs. The following procedure was suggested by a Zen Master: 1) sit comfortably with a straight spine, then try to fill the lower part of your abdomen with air. Of course we know the lungs are elsewhere, but by thinking "low abdomen," you will feel the abdominal muscles move; these muscles control the diaphragm; 2) start exhaling slowly with a thin flow of breath, keeping your spine straight and your breastbone high, then increase the air flow and finish by expelling the air and making a sound, "unh." The purpose of all this is to connect the breath with the diaphragm ("rooted" sound).

Another helpful exercise is to lie flat on your stomach on the floor. Let your right arm lie alongside your body. Put your left arm above your head with the elbow bent. Face into the bent elbow. Relax and then try to groan as if in pain. You will feel the muscles of the abdomen working against the floor. This is a sign that the diaphragm is engaged.

It may seem that we are making too much fuss over the intake of a breath. Some people take it in naturally in the right way; those people need not worry. But if the singer is self-conscious and stiff about the intake of breath, then it is worth any amount of trouble to try to find the free-rooted sound of instantaneous interaction of impulse and diaphragmatic breath.

Once the connection of the breath with the diaphragm is established, the next step is very simple. *Watch* that the breath flows continuously upward and inward to and through the vocal instrument (the larynx, the vocal cords, and the open throat) toward the natural megaphone, the pharynx. The open throat is extremely important. It is best achieved by sensing an inner smile, *not* an imitation of one, but the very delightful feeling which starts deep in the body and makes you want to burst out laughing.

The active part of the work is now over. One now must simply observe the process of the breath flowing upwards. What could be simpler? This is not to say that it is easy, since this simple process is contrary to the usual way of exhaling. We breathe unconsciously all of our lives and we have built very strong habits. To begin with, most of us do not take a low breath; usually we fill just the top part of our lungs, and sometimes the middle. Even if we were to take some time and trouble to establish a low intake of breath, connected with the diaphragm, the long exhaling process would still be new. Very often we exhale from the top, letting the breast-bone drop, which tightens the surrounding muscles and locks the available supply of air so that it cannot be used. When this happens (and it happens often) the singer will complain that there is not enough breath to finish the phrase. Sometimes this occurs during a short phrase—much to the surprise of the singer, who can easily sing long phrases when the breath intake is low and the exhaling starts from the same low point.

There is another important point: breathing is unconscious and constant; it also reflects our state of mind. If we are disturbed, it becomes jerky and uneven. A peaceful state of mind brings with it a smooth flow of breath. Fortunately, there are good ways to control breath in singing. Avoid taking in air mechanically. This is essential. We all have experienced how difficult and even tiring it can be to take a few deep breaths at the request of a doctor. So, since breath reflects our mental state, *take that breath to express the feeling of the musical phrase and text.* The emotional content will stimulate the impulse, and the impulse in turn will control the breath. If your desire to express the phrase is strong, and you feel the urge to sing it through to the very end, your breath control will be good.

6

Speech (Diction)

Speech as a tool in formation of words, like elements of breath and impulse, is usually unconscious. It can, however, be consciously improved or modified.

We usually identify diction as a series of different meaningful sound units, but as a matter of fact it is a combination of the shapes formed mostly by the tongue. To convey meaning, the shapes are of primary importance; we can eliminate sound and shape the words tonelessly and still convey the meaning. When people who are deaf read lips, they are reading shapes. On the other hand, if the shapes are removed or blurred, speech can no longer be understood. So clear and crisp shape formation is essential.

Western speech has two types of formations: open vowels and closed consonants. Since classical singing is done on vowels, our main concern is how to form and maintain them clearly without unnecessary tension. Some personal habits of speech may help or hinder their formation.

Consonants are produced by the action of various surfaces of the vocal apparatus. They do not contribute to sonority, but rather perform in a percussive manner. For good diction it is essential to reproduce the consonants sharply and quickly. Lingering on consonants should be avoided because it may close the throat and stop the flow of breath. Our main concern is with vowels, which are primarily shaped by the thick muscle of the tongue. As we pronounce different vowels, the tongue changes its shape and position. This movement affects the position of the throat which must be kept open for the flow of sound.

People usually find that it is easy to maintain an open position on certain vowels and hard on others; which vowels are easy and which are difficult depends on the individual construction of the vocal apparatus and the habitual manner of speech. There are some lucky people whose throats remain almost continually open through all vowel changes. These are the people who have "naturally placed voices." However, not everyone is so lucky. Two things are helpful: 1) the *true*, inner smile (not an imitation), and 2) the thrust of the tip of the tongue toward the lower teeth, which will keep the thick part of the tongue from sagging down in the throat and interfering with the flow of breath. This forward thrust will help to keep the tongue vital; it is also very important for the lips to be alive. This tongue position together with an inner smile and words crisply formed by vital lips and tip of the tongue give the impression of "singing forward." Using these means, the formation of vowels will flow smoothly, the swiftly executed consonants will not interfere with the melodic line, and the imagination will be free to create the desired music through impulse and concentration.

7

Sound

In order to gain better control of our instrument (the voice) we have tried to understand and isolate its component elements: impulse, breath, and speech. We now come to sound. As a tool, sound is quite different from the other three which we have already discussed. Impulse is present in everything alive, and its different manifestations were pointed out in an earlier discussion. Our task is to become aware of it, recognize it, and use it consciously. Breath we all know well; we breathe from the moment of birth to the last moment of life. We study speech by eliminating sound and shaping words tonelessly, thus sensing more clearly the muscular movements and forms produced by the tongue and lips. In discussing these elements, we are trying to isolate the different components of the vocal process, to become conscious of each one separately and in this way learn to control them.

We cannot apply the same process to sound. Sound is the

sum total—the result of impulse, breath, and speech working together simultaneously. Of course, the complete isolation of the separate functioning parts is very difficult to achieve; the parts affect each other and the most vulnerable part is the sound.

To begin with, each of us is born with our own built-in instrument. Bone structure, cavities, thickness or thinness of muscles, etc. all determine our particular, very individual sonority. This sonority can be modified by good or poor use of impulse, breath, and speech, but the essential sound is a very personal attribute of a singer. In this respect, the singer differs from the instrumentalist. Of course every musician needs to have good sonority to perform good music and quite often talented young instrumentalists do not own good instruments, but for them there is always the hope and very often the chance of acquiring a fine one. The singer's instrument is his for life, and quite understandably he identifies himself with it. This attitude makes it very difficult to be objective in analyzing the other components, particularly if the singer's natural sonority is rich. In such cases the sound, instead of being a means of making music, may become a goal in itself. This attitude is very often supported by the general public. How often do we hear the singer being praised for the phrasing, sensitivity of style, or musicianship? Hardly ever. The usual praise is, "What a beautiful voice!" When the natural, beautiful sound is combined with a well coordinated use of tools no immediate harm results. But sometimes a lovely sound can be produced in spite of the faulty use of tools—then there is trouble. People praise the sound; the singer is reluctant to change anything in spite of danger signals such as flat intonation, short breath, or cracking on high notes, and we watch another "vocal meteor" flashing by and disappearing much too soon from the musical horizon.

The singer who can produce a desirable sound on any pitch at any speed is in control of his technique and ready to use it for the art of singing, provided all nuance changes are made by means of the imagination and do not interfere with the correct use of the tools.

8

The Art of Singing

We will now turn our attention to the Art of Singing: the artistic and musical ideas, their aims, and the means by which to express them. From time immemorial in all countries people have sung, but the standards of beauty and the techniques used have not been the same in different periods and in different countries. The great majority of singers, however, use and depend on the tools which were described in the previous chapters. The following discussion of artistic aims and means is addressed primarily to singers who are soloists, since choral singers are subject to the conductor's ideas and directions and cannot make their own choices.

The diversity of standards, tastes, and traditions in the field of singing is so great that I will limit myself to a very small part of Western classical music from the last few centuries—oratorios, opera, and art songs or lieder. Many professional singers perform in all three categories. Vocally, the requirements are the same in all three: clarity and exactness of pitch and rhythm, all of which depend on control of the singer's tools; but artistically and musically the demands differ.

The demands of oratorio are the least taxing. The solos are often written in an instrumental manner; the vocal line is prominent and the text plays merely a secondary role. Very often the text consists of two or three sentences repeated many times. Of course, there are some exceptions such as the part of the Evangelist in the Bach Passions, but usually the dramatic expression of that text is limited to a few short recitatives.

In opera, the vocal part often demands great range and volume. A dramatic rendition of the text, through which the story unfolds, is also essential, so diction and emotional expression become very important. To compensate for these demands, however, opera provides the singer with a lot of support. Costumes, make-up, scenery, lights, and the acting of the rest of the cast help visually and psychologically in the creation of a role.

The demands of lieder singing are very different from those of opera and oratorio. To begin with, there is the actual amount of singing. Oratorio or opera performances last roughly two to three hours. The time is divided among an orchestral overture, choruses, arias by different soloists, ensembles, possibly a ballet, and several intermissions. The actual singing time for one soloist is from twenty to thirty minutes. The actual singing time in a lieder recital is about eighty minutes.

Another major difference is that while operas and oratorios are sung in one language, it is not unusual to hear lieder in four different languages. On a lieder program, moreover, the groups of songs may belong to different musical periods and therefore demand quick changes from one style to another, something that does not happen in operas or oratorios.

Still more important is the difference found in the relation between music and text. In opera the text is the result of a collaboration between a librettist and a composer. Sometimes they work concurrently; sometimes the music is written before the text. This is not so with lieder. The texts exist first, in the form of poetry. The composer expresses the poetry in musical terms.

The interpretation of such music makes great demands on the artist. The best interpretive musician is like a spotlessly clean mirror which reflects the music of the composer without missing anything in it and without imposing the performer's own personality on it. This is a difficult standard to meet. People have different temperaments, they reflect art according to their own natures: some are dramatic, others lyrical or restrained, and so performances are not flatly uniform but varied and alive. This is both unavoidable and desirable. What should be avoided is the conscious deviation from the composer's intentions (tempi, nuances, etc.).

The best approach to a correct interpretation is to follow in the footsteps of the composer. The composer began with the poetry, so the first thing for the singer to do is to become thoroughly acquainted with the text. Since many of the songs are in languages which the singer may not know well, a considerable amount of time must be spent in making translations. To have a general idea of the meaning is not enough. It is necessary to know and to understand every word in all its shadings.

When the text has been well-absorbed, then it is time to see how the composer has fitted it to the melodic line. Some

composers apparently think singing is intensified and prolonged speech, and their melodic lines fit easily to the rise
and fall of a spoken phrase. Others are less obvious, and
more time must be spent in trying to penetrate that merging
of poetry and music, a unity which exists in any fine composition. Clearly, this merging can occur only in the original
language; to sing lieder in translation is to mutilate them.

I cannot emphasize too strongly the necessity of reading
the music carefully and observing meticulously the markings: forte, piano, all accents, ties, ritardandos, accelerandos,
etc. How often have I heard a student say, "I do not know
what to do with this phrase." Nine times out of ten my
response is, "You have not followed the markings." By
following I do not mean a mechanically accurate rendition; I
mean finding what the real inner need is for the indicated
nuances.

I strongly advise singers not to start actually singing until
all the phrases ring clearly in the mind. This practice will also
clarify the question of where to take a breath. The breath
must be taken because of the urge to express the meaning of
the whole phrase; then the impulse will carry the breath to
the end. When this happens, the intake of breath becomes an
integral part of the singing and not an interruption.

To perform well and accurately and yet keep a sense of
freedom, the singer must know the accompaniment as well
as the vocal part, and hear it uninterruptedly in his imagination throughout the piece. In this imaginative process the
singer sings both the vocal part and the accompaniment; the
impulse leads and unfolds but only the voice is heard.

A special approach is called for in songs which represent
a dialogue: songs like Schubert's "Der Tod und das Mädchen"
and "Erlkönig," Moussorgsky's "Berceuse" from *Songs and*

Dances of Death, or Franz Liszt's "Comment, disaient-ils." The problem is to give an impression of two or more different voices without losing control of vocal guidelines. It is a real test of a singer's technique. Almost always, the first temptation is to fake an entirely difference voice, which involves radically changing the alignment of the instrument. Such a maneuver may be quite effective, but it is very risky, as the singer may not be able to return quickly to the correct alignment. In a song like "Berceuse," the dialogue between the pleading mother and overpowering Death proceeds without pauses, and there is simply no time to maneuver. What the singer has to do in such cases is to become a mimic: He must hear internally, with utmost clarity, the quality of the voice he wants to represent, and at the same time still keep a strong sense of open throat and a flow of breath. The sonority will be different from the singer's usual one and the difference will be emphasized through subtle changes in the manner of speech.

The following experiment is worth trying: Say some phrase such as, "Oh, so you have returned!" in different ways: 1) very joyfully, 2) mockingly, 3) as if you are annoyed, 4) angrily, 5) tearfully. Maintain good vocal alignment and listen for the desired quality. You will notice that your speech is subtly modified with each new mood. This experiment highlights the important role of speech changes. These changes affect the fine nuances and the style.

Style is the area in which a singer, particularly a young singer, often appears at a disadvantage, because of the comparatively short span of his musical life and experience. A gifted young pianist may have started playing at the age of seven or even six, and with good teaching and serious work habits may be ready for public appearances at the age of twenty. By that time he has played a great deal of music and should know the stylistic differences between Mozart, Brahms, Chopin, Debussy, Bartok, etc. But a singer at the age of twenty has had at most two or three years of serious study and has not had time to get acquainted with a large amount of music. So it is understandable if the group of Schumann songs in his concert sounds exactly like the group of Schubert songs. One must know a lot of music in order to have a sense of musical style.

When young singers start to learn a work by a composer who is comparatively new to them, I advise them to listen to as many recordings of this composer's works as possible, and not to confine their listening to vocal compositions. When listening to a vocal recording, it is a wise precaution to follow the score. All too often, famous singers take liberties with the music, and it is necessary to remember that these famous people are great *in spite of* these liberties, and not to imitate their interpretations.

During a performance, what should be the focus of the singer's attention? What should he concentrate on? Ideally he should concentrate on the *essence of the poetic meaning of the text*. In a way it is the "beginning of the beginning," and therefore the heart of the song, which brings us once again to the impulse.

As we know, strong concentration results in a great influx of energy-impulse. If a singer is preoccupied with sonority, then sonority will flourish and such a singer may become a great vocalist whose place may be in opera. If, however, the singer is more interested in musical phrasing, nuances, and the poetry of the text, then the object of concentration may become less clear. The mental process brings complications and to some extent, dissipates the necessary concentration.

To avoid this, the singer must hear the song in imagination as if it were being performed by an ideal artist: for sonority, text, speech, musical structure from the first note of the accompaniment to the last, all the poetic and musical meaning. It is a difficult task, but it is worthwhile to have it as a goal. One thing is clear: such work takes time. It is simply impossible to do quickly. Some people learn and memorize very easily, but that is the process of active thought. I am speaking of the process of imagination which silences thought.

When the imagination is engaged, the song unfolds freely with no mental effort, and almost sings itself. The sensation is of release and of wonderful freedom. Once a very gifted student of mine was working on some phrase which sounded a little stilted. After a few tries, the voice soared beautifully. The student finished the phrase, burst into tears and then said, "Nothing is wrong. I am so happy. The feeling of freedom is unbelievable!" This feeling of freedom is the reward for all struggles which strew the path of a singer.

But the process of imagination requires time and solitude. Everyday life becomes more and more fragmented; so many contacts, so many activities to choose from, jobs, obligations, distractions—there is hardly ever a long enough stretch of peaceful time, the kind of time which is necessary for any artistic activity. Creative artists, composers, writers, painters, do their work in solitude and peace. Everybody accepts and respects this fact. The same conditions, although perhaps not as much time, are also a necessity for the interpretive artist.

To be able to interpret a song means to be able to come as close as possible to the state of mind in which it was created by the composer and the poet. Practicing and memorizing are necessary, but they produce only the "blueprint," and not yet the living thing. To breathe life into a song, one must run through it many times in one's imagination, silently, without making any audible sounds. If the days are so filled with various duties that there is not enough time to do this, then a couple of sleepless nights must be spent in order to get this essential work done.

One often hears perfectly correct performances which do not leave a lasting memory. With the help of copying machines and recordings, new music is easily distributed and there are many bright singers who are able to learn difficult rhythms and intervals quickly—so a lot of new music is heard. Quite often it is performed with the score in hand. To hear a performance like that is like looking at a snapshot of an unfamiliar place—it is not vivid and the impression soon fades. These songs are rarely repeated after the first performance.

Sometimes such performances are unavoidable, but I would call these the *job* **of** singing, not the art of singing. As a matter of fact, the real musical-artistic work begins only *after* a song is completely memorized; then the performer can use his imagination freely, while always adhering to the composer's indications. I feel that with some rare exceptions the singer should try very hard to feel, hear, and understand the composer's intentions. It takes time.

I would hope that this attitude would eliminate many of the so-called "traditions" which usually stem from some liberties taken by some famous singers. These may be rather musically charming deviations, and skillfully executed, but after a time, imitations by less gifted singers become exaggerations and give the impression of an alien and coarse growth on the fine musical body of the song.

The kind of interpretive work I have been discussing may

be very tedious for some people and most rewarding for others. It depends entirely on the character of the person performing. If the main interest lies in self-gratification, then this work will be unpleasant. If, however, the main interest of a singer is to serve music, then the reward of the discipline provides a great freedom in which the song sings itself.

9

Teaching

Many colleges which give a degree in the performance of music and offer courses in the "methodology" of singing. Any method implies a set of prescribed activities. It leaves very little room for an individual approach and inevitably results in rather mediocre efficiency. It may be of some help in the first stages of instrumental studies, but try as I may, I cannot see anything but harm in a "method" applied to a singer. As I mentioned in the first chapter, there are "natural" singers with very little or no training at all who have long and successful careers. Since singing is an organic and therefore a "natural" process, I think we should try to understand and emulate the physical and psychological process of these natural singers.

I do not mean to say that achieving a "natural" singing style is easy or requires little time and effort. On the contrary, to those who wish to put into practice the ideas set forth in this book, I must issue a warning: The approach described here requires a great deal of work and concentration. It is not intended for those who want to sing only for a pastime. It is also not meant for those who primarily seek to "please the public." The ideas I outline take no notice of fashion or of the steps one follows to make a career. Rather, I speak to and for those who wish only to pursue excellence and produce beautiful and varied music, and who are interested in the art of singing for its own sake.

When we consider the fact that singing is an organic process, how much analytical thinking and information is helpful? Not too much, particularly for beginners. Learning to sing is like learning to speak a new language. To start by just speaking and then correct obvious mistakes along the way is much better than to start by learning grammatical rules. Somehow the second method, although it produces correct sentences, never allows the language to come to life. Similarly, all artificial positions of an exaggeratedly erect body and all abnormal manipulations of the mouth—contrary to clear speech—produce stiff, unmusical phrases. Obviously a good position of the body, the head, and the neck—that is, the whole alignment of our instrument—is very important. What is the best position? One very often hears advice "to relax." Undoubtedly it is better to relax than to be stiff, but relaxation is not the whole answer. I would like, once more, to call attention to the gymnast getting ready to perform: the spine is straight but not stiff, the knees are slightly loose, the chest bone is high, the shoulders are *not* pulled back, and the head rests on top of the spine freely with the chin slightly in. The body feels strong and free and provides a good channel through which the vital force, the impulse, can flow.

Some people respond readily and easily to corrections of

a physical nature; others are self-conscious and respond but slightly to such suggestions. My experience is that initially it is best to be satisfied with small improvements. Too much insistence on changes in posture may only increase self-consciousness. If the student has severe problems with general relaxation and physical awareness, exercises such as swimming may be useful.

In my experience, the most helpful way to begin the study of singing is to have the pupil sing a simple song, to select the best-sounding phrase and point it out. Do not hesitate to praise the pupil if he deserves it. Ask him to repeat the good phrase. Explain *why* it sounded better than the rest, and work from there into the rest of the song.

The position of the jaw is extremely important. Contrary to the opinion of most singers, it should not be "dropped." Singers need to open the top of the throat without pulling down the larynx. The desirable position can be formed by a deep inner smile bordering on the feeling of laughter. It is impossible to sustain a smile when the jaw is dropped. Dropping the jaw is usually an attempt to release a tension in the neck and the back of the tongue, which can be a serious obstacle to singing. On the other hand, the position of the jaw, when there is an inner smile, makes the crisp formation of words in the front of the mouth easy and natural while at the same time it relaxes the neck and the back of the tongue. This way of forming words—with the tip of the tongue and with live lips while keeping an inner smile—improves diction immediately. It eliminates unnecessary "mouthing" and helps miraculously with the pronunciation of foreign languages. It gives the impression of the voice being produced "forward." Being conscious of the tip of the tongue prevents the back of the tongue from constricting the throat and leaves the throat comfortably open for sound.

So, when the impulse is strong, breath flows continuously through the open throat, speech is crisp and forward, the instrument is well aligned. But here again a complication arises which instrumentalists do not encounter. The impulse which tunes our vocal instrument keeps it in a state of constantly changing tension. This change is sensed by the singer and sometimes interferes with maintaining the alignment of the instrument. Instrumentalists do not have this problem. The state of their instruments does not change. We may compare an instrumentalist to a dancer on a steady floor and a singer to a person trying to balance on a rocking boat.

Obviously, singers and instrumentalists have different problems; the same type of exercises do not fulfill the same kind of function for the two groups. Yet in music schools singers are given exercises similar to those designed for instrumentalists, such as scales, arpeggios, staccato, jumps, etc. All of this is of no help to singers in maintaining the necessary coordination and creates the false impression that singers have to do something special and different every time they see a new pattern in music. Such techniques are instrumental, intended for dealing with the location of notes. The singer who uses this approach forgets the marvelous creative roles of imagination and impulse and begins blindly to manipulate the "voice" as if it were a tangible object. This is not to say that there is not technique to singing, but it is *not analogous to the technique for other instruments.*

I prefer not to use any exercises with beginners at the start, because at this point they are more or less confused about the tools of singing. Until a certain degree of sensitivity to the components of singing has been developed, exercises are of no use. Later on, students should try the following exercises which are very helpful: 1) change vowels on one note, and see that it is done with the tip of the tongue thrust forward so that the throat stays open and the flow of breath is continuous. Then do the same exercise on different pitches. 2) On one vowel sing the following arpeggio: (*up*) do mi sol do mi sol (*and then down*) fa re si sol fa re do. Keep the vowel sound clear all the time, and particularly watch that the breath still flows up as the pitch moves down. Do it in different keys. If the pupil can do these exercises really well, there is no need to spend more time on them. The use of the tools will remain the same in any case and the rest depends on clarity of hearing and acute self-observation and awareness.

Impulse, sound, breath, and speech constitute our tools. When these components work well together, the result is a well-aligned instrument. The ability to keep an alignment in spite of the changes of pitch, mood, and volume demanded by the music constitutes the singer's skill. *This is the technique of the singer.*

But the most perfect alignment cannot by itself produce music. In order to produce a song, the singer must have it clearly in mind: pitch, rhythm, musical form, and the emotional content of the words. *The performer is the imagination.*

Many teachers put great emphasis on reading music well. It is, of course, necessary to read music well in order to sing for pay. All singers must eat, so reading well in order to earn money by singing in a church choir or a chorus is necessary. But reading music is a function that does not include imagination and, in fact, interferes with the process of singing. As a line of notes is read the breath tends to move up and down with the printed line; a movement that is contrary to the continuous upward flow of breath needed to produce a full sound. When a student reads musical notation, the intellectual process, and not the imagination, predominates. But in ideal singing, the whole musical idea exists in the imagination. The actual singing merely releases what is already heard in the internal ear. At such a moment the singer is truly free. In order to sing in this way, the music must be memorized. Singers must also get used to memorizing many songs in different languages, not just a few arias and songs in one language. Once the music is memorized, it is possible to begin to work towards the flexibility and breadth of musical approach that an interpretive artist has to have.

To achieve a high level of continuous, conscious concentration on music and yet keep track of physical coordination requires a great deal of self-observation. Of course, coordination can happen "by the grace of God" in a moment of inspiration, but one cannot count on that, so we must try to be self-observant. After long years of teaching, I have come to the conclusion that the most gifted singers are the least self-observant. These singers are no more interested in analysis of difficulties than very healthy people in lectures on health. Natural singers instinctively do the right, or nearly right, thing in order to sing well; but when something goes wrong they become frustrated and try blindly to "doctor up" the situation. Such singers are reached more quickly by symbols or analogies than by an analytic approach.

The singers who respond best to a concrete approach to vocal production, i.e. control of different components, are usually the ones who have had some experience in professional work, that is to say, work under all sorts of conditions and pressures. Their response is immediate and gratifying.

What about the many people who have nice voices, like to

sing, have no special goals or ambition, but would like to improve their singing? The best thing for them to do is to follow the guidelines that were given before. It is extremely important for singers to sing a song which they really like and are comfortable with. At this stage of development it is preferable for the song to be in a familiar language. Then the singer should ask this question, "Which part of me is the performer and which part is the instrument?" The performer is the imagination. If the imagination is to work freely, the mind must be uncluttered. Everything except the song must fall away. As for the instrument: What happens in the body when the vocal process is good? There is a low intake of breath, a continuous exhaling toward the pharynx, an open throat, and a crisp speech produced by vital lips and tip of the tongue. Simple as it is, this approach almost immediately frees the voice, increasing both range and volume.

Whenever a student sings this way the reaction is always the same. An incredulous, happy look comes over the singer's face followed by the exclamation, "But this is unbelievable. It's so easy!"

10

Practicing

It is natural that in learning a new activity we have to think about the physical actions which are involved; but as long as these actions depend on conscious thought, the technique will not be reliable. Generally speaking, the acquisition of any technique involves the formation of habits. These habits then allow us to move directly to the physical sensations without requiring any conscious thought. As the muscles are trained in a certain way, new physical sensations develop. We have to become familiar with these sensations and rely on them. This is equally true for instrumentalists and singers, but though the principle is the same, the application is quite different.

What about daily exercises? Instrumentalists practice every day for hours. There are many graded exercises and studies which move steadily from simple to more complicated instrumental technical problems. The goal of these exercises is to strengthen, develop, and refine the instrumentalist's tools—

fingers, lips, etc. The instrumentalist uses and trains fingers, arms, lips, and other muscles—muscles which are *voluntarily* used throughout life. To play an instrument these muscles must be consciously trained to perform new or different work.

A singer tries to train the parts of the vocal instrument which have been used *unconsciously* throughout life (breath, sound, speech) to do the same work but in a different manner, *consciously*. Good or bad practicing by an instrumentalist does not affect the instrument; it stays intact. But when a singer practices badly it can destroy the alignment of the vocal instrument. An instrumentalist can build and control the necessary muscles by practicing the prescribed exercises for hours. But a singer's practice must be in short time spans. Prolonged exercises inevitably result in falling into old habits of *unconscious* use of the vocal tools and blur the self-observation which is so necessary in singing.

Singers have only one tool which can withstand continuous, prolonged practicing: speech. With a little special attention, the tongue and lips can become conscious tools. By eliminating sound and shaping words tonelessly, attention can be focused on the sensation of the physical forms of speech. This process can be practiced anywhere, anytime. There is no need for a studio or a piano. It is only necessary to read soundlessly anything that one sees: signs on the street, labels on products, etc. The goal is not to *develop* anything new, but to become conscious of the process.

In the chapter on teaching I described two simple exercises which help to bring the sensations of the open throat and the upward flow of breath into full consciousness. Unlike the beneficial effects of practicing for instrumentalists, more complicated exercises are of no help to singers. Such exercises distract the singer's attention, which should properly be focused only on physical sensations. Therefore, such exercises are not only a waste of time but can be more harmful than helpful.

How should a singer practice the low intake of breath and its connection to the diaphragm? I know of no exercise: What is needed is an experimental procedure. Aim at low breath intake and a continuous exhaling toward the main resonator, the inner smile. At the same time maintain a straight spine and a high position of the chest bone. I described two examples of ways to work in the chapter on breath. Once this low intake of breath is mastered and the diaphragm is working, it becomes very important to pay close attention to the physical sensation that this kind of breathing engenders. Try to evoke this sensation *in a relaxed way* two or three times—*do not hurry*. It is not advisable to repeat this procedure too many times. Somehow, inevitably, tension sets in and this spoils the whole process. Therefore, repeat the process after some time has elapsed and see if the sensation can be regained without any preliminary exercises.

Impulse and sound do not lend themselves to this kind of practicing. The first step in learning to control impulse is to become aware of it. Imagine that it fills your body. Try to walk lightly, energetically; then for contrast walk heavily, dragging your feet. The difference will be obvious. You should be able to sense how the imagination directs impulse. Make gestures with your hands and arms with a similar intent and now try to make a "rooted" sound. Once you become aware of impulse it will not be difficult to control the diaphragmatic breath.

Now your singer's tools are ready, and it is possible to work on the music. But before you begin this, remember that the singer's instrument, like other instruments, demands a certain amount of maintenance. It is well to remember that unless you make a careful periodic check to see that the tools are functioning correctly, there is a real danger of slipping back into the old *unconscious* habits, which were built up during a whole lifetime.

When your tools are in reasonably good order and you are quite familiar with the music and text, spend some time singing it *silently* in your imagination while moving your lips and tongue in toneless speech with an open throat, and using your *impulse-energy* for the flow of breath. In other words, sing it completely, *but with no sound.* After a short while you will feel you *must* sing it aloud. Do it then. I think you will be happily surprised at how good the result will be.

Do not start to sing until you know the music. Learn short sections well, but do not sight-read at this point, for it is all too easy to forget all about speech and breath and fall into old unconscious habits. Invariably this process is filled with many small difficulties, most of which are completely avoidable.

Never begin to practice or rehearse by working on something that presents difficulties. Starting a practice session with difficult passages is another unhappy inheritance from instrumentalists. They can work this way because they are not in danger of misusing their instrument—something that happens so often to singers.

In general, many difficulties could be eliminated if we could accept the fact that a singer's technique is not similar to an instrumentalist's. In some respects it has more in common with an athlete's training; that is to say, one keeps the elements in perfect form and coordination. When this approach works well, a most extraordinary thing happens. All difficulties disappear, and what used to present a problem "sings itself" without any effort. As a matter of fact, many difficulties are psychological in origin. Something seems difficult because it looks difficult on the printed page of music and distracts our attention from watching form. Then, instead of imagination working, confused and apprehensive thoughts arise; the breath loses its smoothness and the happy coordination of flow is gone.

What are the practical steps which will insure the coordinated use of the singer's tools? The steps are the same as in every technique.

1) You must know what to use and how, and remember how it is done—in other words, *think.*

2) Be very observant of the sensations which result from the proper use of your tools and remember these sensations. Singers must pay close attention, because the correct sensations are very subtle. The flow of breath gives a feeling of a pleasant release not unlike stretching. The top of the back of the throat feels "roomy" and cool when air is drawn through the mouth with an inner smile. The vital tip of the tongue becomes "intelligent," as it is when you send it to investigate the rough edge of a tooth. In other words *you bring consciousness* to the parts of your instrument which you used all your life unconsciously.

3) The last technical step is the same for all performers. It is the "awareness." Instead of thinking and sensing, you become *aware* of all the functioning parts, and you are free to make the music.

A certain amount of nervousness is felt by most performers, particularly young ones. With a well-aligned instrument and attention centered on the music, initial nervousness usually passes quickly. However, I have known cases where in spite of being well prepared from every point of view, singers could not control their nerves and their performances were ruined.

The problem is a lack of concentration. To perform means to have nothing on one's mind but the music. This concentration is like a head-light of a car on a dark road, the road being the music. Turn the light off and accidents can happen in the darkness. Above all, avoid thinking about yourself. It is enough to be instrument and performer; do not be critic and audience at the same time.

11

Program Making

Not enough attention is given to the important consideration of program making, especially programs for public
performances or debut recitals in major cities. Performances
usually cost a fortune, and the hope and goal of these
enterprises is to get the good newspaper reviews which are
so much needed at the beginning of a singer's professional
life.

Naturally, the program must consist of pieces which the
singer likes for their musical value, but the arrangement of
these pieces may help or impair the general impression of the
concert. I have heard programs which consisted entirely of a
singer's favorite pieces for sentimental reasons, and such
programs are all right for informal concerts. However, if one
expects critics to cover the concert, then one has to remember
that the critics go to many concerts, sometimes two or three
in the same day. This means they may hear only the first or
last part of any given concert. Because of the number of

concerts that critics hear, their enthusiasm and interest are not so high as an ordinary concert-goer's, so the program has to appeal to the critics by providing a special interest. It can be done by including in the program some major works such as Alban Berg's *Seven Early Songs*, Debussy's *Cinq Poèmes de Baudelaire*, Ravel's *Chansons Madécasses*, Moussorgsky's *Songs and Dances of Death*, etc., or by arranging groups of songs in such a way that the groups provide contrasts.

In the middle of the twentieth century, most programs started with Handel arias or old Italian songs—it was sort of a "warm up" group for a singer, and I think both the public and critics accepted it. Artistically, this group seemed to be the least interesting. It would be a bad risk to start a recital in this manner nowadays. The critic may have time to stay just for the first group!

The best way to start a program is with the piece which gives you the freest, most secure feeling—something that "sings itself." Add to it three more songs by the same composer, followed by your major work and then the inter-mission. If you have a "first performance" piece, a good place for it is right after the intermission. The last group can be of a virtuoso character, or if it is possible to have an instrumen-tal ensemble such as a string quartet, then you have a wonderful "finale." There are many good works for voice and instruments. Schoenberg's Second String Quartet with the soprano part in the two last movements is a glorious thing.

Some people feel that compositions on the program should follow in chronological order. That may be good for school performances, but such an order creates unnecessary limita-tions. What is desirable in a program is a certain amount of control and freshness of impression. If there is a group of unrelated songs it is advisable to check tonalities, so that the audience will not be disturbed by hearing three songs in succession in F major. Except for a cycle like *Die Schoene Muellerin* of Schubert, it is difficult to present a whole evening of one composer's songs—difficult for the performer to do and for the public to listen to. For a young singer, it is better to avoid such programming.

Other types of programs are seen occasionally, such as one made up of songs which all have dance titles: waltzes, mazurkas, minuets, etc. This program may look like fun on paper. However, listening to it proves disappointing—after hearing two or three waltzes you really have had enough! The second kind of program presents different composers who use the same text: poems of Verlaine set to music by Debussy and by Fauré or poems of Goethe with music by Beethoven, Schumann, Liszt, etc. This kind of program may be of real interest to musicologists, or in a classroom. Listening to this program, one begins to compare, choose, analyze. The very nature of such presentations demands mental activity. This is fine in itself, but does not produce an aesthetic impression: the real goal of performance.

Unless it is specially required, a program made up of entirely new, contemporary music is better avoided. Listening to new music requires real concentration on the part of the listener. To concentrate this way for over an hour's time is really too much to ask, even from a musical public. People have argued with me on this subject, saying that such a program is like an exhibition of new paintings and that the public constantly goes to such exhibitions. The difference between an exhibition and a concert is that you can walk through the exhibition at your own pace, stop when a work attracts you, and return as many times as you like to something that catches your attention. You cannot do this at a concert. There are moments that particularly please you and you wish you could dwell on them, but the music is already gone. I have always thought it would be wonderful for musicians who present brand new music to choose fewer pieces and perform them *twice* on the program. It would give the public a chance to get really acquainted with the pieces.

Finally, the young performer should plan the program carefully, allowing plenty of time for rehearsals and for gaining complete knowledge of the music. Instead of starting with a random assortment of pieces and a concert date, the singer should carefully shape the program and allow for sufficient practice time. The conditions would then be right for a fine aesthetic experience.

12

Conclusion

After all this practical advice, I'd like to make a general observation not only on singing but also on all music making at the present time.

Besides learning and performing the standard repertoire, young artists feel constantly obliged to perform unknown pieces: either contemporary pieces with only their newness to recommend them or unknown pieces by well-known composers (unknown because they are not good). It has to be new, a first performance.

With the development of technology (compact discs, records, tapes, radio and television performances, photocopies, etc.), we are inundated with all sorts of music: classical, popular, folk, rock—anything you want. Some are great performances; some are mediocre; some are bad. Music is heard everywhere: at home, at the beach, in the car, at the market, at parties, and coming from empty apartments—people go out and leave their radios on. Our ears are saturated with sound, and if we hear a new performance (either a new piece of music or a familiar one performed by a new artist), we are really not in a perceptive state to judge the quality. The quantity of music blunts the sensitivity to quality. I find it a great problem of our time—quantity versus quality.

Museums and concert halls are crowded with eager people who want to see and hear the beauty revealed to creative artists but hidden from ordinary people. In museums the viewersreact directly to the work. How strong and lasting the work's impact is depends on the quality of the work and the sensitivity of the viewer.

In concert halls the situation is quite different: the most extraordinary musical score is useless unless there are interpretive artists to perform it. These artists are responsible to a certain degree for the success or failure (particularly in first performances) of compositions. The performers must be skillful, sensitive, and sympathetic to the performed piece. I feel that the greatest reward after a concert is when people say, "Those songs are incredibly beautiful."

Apart from these conditions, there are other problems: time, money, and a place are needed for rehearsals. If the composition is for a large group of performers, the price of rehearsals gets so forbidding that only one rehearsal is possible. This *does* happen. If the performers are experienced musicians, the performance will be smooth and people usually will say "it was a good performance." But this is not enough to be a "memorable" performance. The sad thing is that memorable performances are rare, even when well-known artists are performing. The famous musical organizations, opera companies, orchestras, and ensembles, constantly perform with hardly any time to rest while we, the public, expect the performances to be inspired!

Before airplanes became the main means of transport, there was time between engagements, and even if it was spent on travel, there was a sense of rest and relaxation. The number of engagements was much smaller and there was no feeling of meeting "the deadline." Performing was a happy event.

I wish I had a practical solution to our present situation. I do not. I only know that a large amount of music, hastily done, is very unfair to performers, robbing them of the necessary conditions for doing their best—something they are quite capable of, provided the time is there.

Singing is an expression of life, and if you have no time for your life, how can you sing? Quality always needs time, not only in music but also in life itself.